Financial Facts for Females

Questions, Answers, and Actions

Celvia Stovall, Ph.D.

TENNESSEE VALLEY
Publishing®

Knoxville, Tennessee
2004

Published by Tennessee Valley Publishing
PO Box 52527 Knoxville, TN 37950-2527

Printed in the United States of America

Library of Congress Control Number: 2004112523

ISBN: 1-932604-13-8

Cover Designed by: Kimberly J. Stallings

Celvia Stovall, PhD

Acknowledgments

I am grateful to the many women that trusted me to work with them during difficult financial times. Their stories and my personal experiences have inspired me to commit a portion of my life to helping women make a difference in their financial life.

To my family, friends, and co-workers, words are inadequate to describe the love and support you have extended me. Your prayers and encouragement never allowed me to give up, even when I thought I had good excuses to do so.

My sincerest appreciation is extended to my Tennessee Valley Publishing family. You are the BEST! You have been my cheering squad since 1999. Your kind words and quality service has meant the world to me. I will forever consider myself a part of your family.

Last, but certainly not least, To God I give all the glory. Without Him the second printing of this book would never have become a reality.

Contents

Introduction

Over the past few years I have had the opportunity to meet and work with a diverse group of females facing serious financial dilemmas. These females, whether family, friends, co-workers, church members, students or clients, have asked me why most books about money are so intimidating and hard to understand. They want books and learning materials that will answer their questions and help them develop sound financial skills. These females from all walks of life struggle daily with money issues. Their money issues are both believable and unbelievable, but all the females have one thing in common, they desire a sense of control when it comes to managing money. As I reflect over these issues, I am reminded that:

Some are in abusive situations and fearful of leaving because they cannot financially afford to leave.

Some qualify to retire because of age and years of service, but cannot do so because they have not saved for retirement.

Some retired, but have to return to the work force because their retirement income is inadequate.

Some had a spouse that passed away and did not have the proper legal documents in place.

Some hate their jobs, but cannot afford to make a change.

Some have a spouse or partner with a serious drug addiction and are on the verge of losing everything they have worked for.

Some have to postpone or give up their dream of a college education because they are in excessive debt.

Some are embarrassed because creditors are calling them at work and they do not have the money to stop the calls.

Some are going through a divorce and for the first time realized what his income REALLY is.

Some do not know their spouse's income and are afraid to ask.

Some are in so much debt they pawn their jewelry regularly to pay living expenses.

Some withdrawn funds from their IRAs and pay a financial penalty, because they need the money to pay bills.

Some dare not bring up the subject of money in the house or ask any questions about it.

Some worked hard, but never buy anything for themselves because they feel guilty.

Some do not know the amount of their household debt because they are not allowed to open credit statements that come in the mail.

Some have annual household incomes over $100,000 a year and cannot save $1,000.

Some say they would be embarrassed if their family and friends really knew how they lived financially.

Some have extended family members depending on them financially and they are struggling themselves.

The females described above are running scared and do not know what to do when it comes to their financial lives. Ten years ago it would have been difficult for me to believe money could cause so much trauma in the lives of females. Today, I support the statement, "money is a matter of life or death." I personally know females who have lost families, jobs, and lives, because of finances.

We have become a society too focused on titles and on things. We define ourselves and our successes by the amount of money we make and the kind of things we are able to accumulate. Almost everything we do revolves around money, but too few really know how to manage it or how to make it work for us. Money is a tool. It is a resource to help us reach our goals.

Romans 12:2 reads, "And be not conformed to this world: but be ye transformed by the renewing of your mind, that ye may prove what is good, and acceptable, and perfect, will of God." God's desire is for us to have the BEST. However, receiving the best often requires us to change our mind and our actions.

It is my prayer that God will use me as a vessel to address financial facts that all females should know. My goals is to present information in an easy to understand format that will help females change the way they think about financial resources and how they use them.

Financial Facts for Females provides answers and actions to common money problems. If practiced, the information in this book can change your life.

Chapter One
Females And Finances: The Statistical Facts

Did you know:
Ninety percent (90%) of females can expect to be alone at some point in their life. Divorce, death of a spouse and the decision to remain single will require women to learn how to manage money to get the things they need and want in life.

Females, on the average, outlive males. A female's life expectancy is 79 years, compared to 72 years for males. Therefore, females should not expect their spouses to be around to support them until their death.

Females head over 50% of households in America. Many of these households are not receiving child support and thus are in poverty status.

Females in America earn less than 80% of every dollar males earn. Although the income gap between males and females is getting closer, males continue to make more money than females.

Females world-wide earn less than males. In Bangladesh, females earn 42% of what males earn. In Chile, females earn 61% of what males earn, and in the Arab Republic, females earn 65% of what males earn.

Females receiving social security benefits, on the average, receive 37% less than males. Social Security benefits are based on income during the employment years. Therefore since females earn less, they can expect less social security.

Females on the average, receive less than $600 a month in social security.

Females are more likely to work outside the home. Current statistics indicate that over 60% of females today are in the labor force. Many of these females are employed in minimum wage positions that do not allow them to move their families out of poverty.

Females with higher education and the ability to work long hours are more likely to be able to keep their family out of poverty after a divorce than are females without these attributes.

Females are likely to live in poverty during their senior years. Statistics indicate that 80% of Americans live in poverty during retirement. Seventy percent (70%) of elderly females live in poverty.

Females change jobs more often than males. Females over 25 years old of age change jobs every 4.8 years compared to males changing every 6.6 years.

Females are less likely than males to worry about retirement and to invest for it. On the average, females save less, and start saving later. They also use savings and investment instruments that are conservative and offer low fixed rates of return.

Females' standard of living is likely to decrease 27%-45% after a divorce while the average males standard of living increases 10%-15%.

Females, married and single, employed outside the home say that their income is necessary. Sixty-four percent (64%) of working females indicate that their income covers half or more of the total household expenses.

Females are more likely to be employed in positions that lack retirement benefits and health coverage. One out of every three females work in positions without retirement benefits or sick leave, and three out of ten are employed in positions without medical coverage.

Females are more likely than males to be employed by companies in low paying positions. Thirty-three percent (33%) of the women in the United States are employed in such positions.

Females working outside the home are likely to hold multiple jobs. Statistics indicate that the percentage of women holding more than one job grew from 20% in 1973 to 47% in 1995.

Females are responsible for 85% of household spending. Therefore, it is imperative that they have knowledge of how to get the most for their money.

So what do these statistical facts mean?

The statistical facts about females and finances provides more than factual, startling, and eye opening information. These facts should serve as a wake-up call to all women regardless of marital status, economic status, race, age or geographical location. Women more than ever before should realize:

We can no longer afford to depend on a spouse or significant other for financial security. For years we have waited on our knight in shining armor to financially rescue us. We must decide that we will personally take responsibility for our lives, including how we manage our money.

We must learn the importance of preparing for the future. We cannot wisely meet future needs if we fail to save and invest today.

We must learn the financial language and become comfortable speaking it. Remember, it is okay to ask questions and identify resources to assist us until we can handle it alone.

We must learn that there is a difference between wants and needs, and too many wants can leave us with too little money to meet our needs.

We must learn how to use credit and not let it use us.

We must learn the value of an education. Education and job readiness can make a financial difference.

We must learn that it is never too late to learn how to manage money. Now is a great time to get started.

We have learned to work for money, but most of us have not learned how to make money work for us. That mentality will stop today. We will start this day, working on ways to change some of the negative statistics that describe female money management. We can break through the glass ceiling that prevents financial success. Our track record shows we have prevailed before, and we will do it again - Financially!

 **Action**

1. Do you see yourself in any of the statistics cited?

2. If yes to #1, have you thought about what you can do to change your situation?

3. List three goals you would like to achieve as a result of reading this book.

   1. Debt Free

   2. Emergency savings

   3. Financial stability 4ever + there after for my children

A woman's best security is her own money.

Chapter Two
Your Financial Worth

I f someone asked you what you were worth in dollars and cents, would you be able to tell them? Most females do not know their financial net worth. Your financial net worth is what you have left when you subtract all your debts from all your assets (or the things you own). All females, regardless of marital status, should know their financial net worth.

Why do females need to know their financial worth?

Statistical facts indicate that 90% of all females can expect to be the household financial decision maker at some point in their life. As a result, they must understand finances and be prepared to make sound financial decisions. Knowing your financial worth is a great place to start your financial education. The process one goes through to determine financial worth will assist in understanding:

- the value of all personal property
- total debt amount
- if adequate funds are being saved for retirement, education, or other goals
- if there is enough insurance coverage and
- if it is possible to qualify for a loan if needed

Will a female's financial worth always be the same?

No, financial net worth will likely increase or decrease each year. Females should however, set a goal each year to increase their net worth by 3-5 percent. Two ways to increase net worth:

- decrease debt
- increase savings

How can I increase my net worth by decreasing debt and increasing savings if my income remains the same?

Using the same income to decrease debt and increase savings will require some creativity and commitment, but it can be done. First, track your spending to see where your money goes. Try using a pocket notepad to write down how you use money every day. Once you know where your money is going, identify ways to change how you spend.

10 ways to decrease debt and save

- use cash instead of credit cards
- email or write instead of calling long distance
- plan meals before shopping and purchase only what you need
- never grocery shop when you are hungry
- know the layout of the stores where you shop and avoid going down each aisle
- increase minimum payments; sending $1-$5 extra can make a difference

- pay bills before due date to avoid late fees and decrease interest charges
- start a family coin collection jar; ask family members to add loose coins weekly
- if you eat out every weekend, give up one weekend and save the money
- commit to only purchasing items on sale

Should females strive to have a specific net worth goal?

Yes. Strive for the highest net worth possible. A good rule is to use your age and income as a guide. Multiply your annual income by your age and divide by 10. Your total is an estimate of what you may want to strive for as a personal net worth goal.

Example:
Age 30. Income $25,000.

Net worth goal:

Step 1: $ 25,000.00
x   30.00
$750,000.00

Step 2: $750,000.00
÷   10.00
$ 75,000.00

What is the best way for females to determine their financial worth?

The best way for females to determine their financial worth is to write it down. Complete a financial net worth statement or financial balance sheet. This document will take an hour or two to complete, but once completed, it will become one of your most valuable documents. Financial net worth statements should be updated each year around the same time of the year. A good time to update is around tax time, since it will require going through important papers.

What important papers are needed to complete a financial net worth statement?

Any papers used to document property or assets owned that give an accurate account of debt amounts owed, are needed to complete the statement. Two lists will be developed during the process. One list will include all assets (what you own) and the other will include liabilities (what you owe). In most cases, you will have all of the information needed. In other cases, a simple phone call is needed to get financial information. The list below can serve as a guide when completing a personal financial net worth statement.

Information needed to complete a net worth statement

All the things you own to include:
- Cash on hand (amount of money in wallet, purse, home piggy banks)
- Bank/Credit Union Statement (checking, savings, CDs, etc.) - use recent statement.
- Investment statements (stocks, bonds, mutual funds, retirement funds, 401(K), etc. - use recent statement or call the investment company.
- Life Insurance cash value
- Home equity
- Vehicle equity
- Value of household furnishings

- Value of all personal property (clothing, jewelry, furs, etc)
- Value of all art, coins, collectibles

All the things you owe to include:
- Credit card debt – use recent statements
- Home mortgage balance
- Second mortgage balance
- Vehicle loan balances
- Installment loan balances
- Education loan balances
- Finance company loan balances
- Outstanding taxes owed
- Loans to other people

Can financial net worth be negative?

Yes. One can have a negative net worth. The main cause of a negative net worth is having more liabilities, or debt, than assets, or things you own. Many females may find themselves with negative net worth, but your net worth does not have to remain negative. Increase net worth by decreasing use of credit, increasing creditor payments and the amount saved regularly.

Financial Net Worth Statement

Date:

ASSETS (Things you own)
Cash on hand . . . . _____
Money in Bank/Credit Union . . . . _____
Money Invested . . . . _____
(stocks, bonds, mutual funds, retirement funds, 401(K)) . . _____
Life Insurance cash value . . . . _____
Home equity . . . . _____
Vehicle equity . . . . _____
Value of household furnishings . . . . _____
Value of all personal property (clothing, jewelry, furs, etc) . _____
Value of all art, coins, collectibles . . . . _____
Other (list items) . . . . _____
        I. Total Assets (things owned) . . . . _____
LIABILITIES (Things you owe for) . . . . _____
Total of all credit card outstanding balances . . . . _____
Home mortgage balance . . . . _____
Second mortgage balance . . . . _____
Vehicle loan balances . . . . _____
Installment loan balances . . . . _____
Education loan balances . . . . _____
Finance company loan balances . . . . _____
Outstanding taxes owed . . . . _____
Money owed to family or friends . . . . _____
Other (list items) . . . . _____
        II. Total Liabilities (things you owe) . . . . _____

Total assets - Total liabilities = Financial Net Worth
_____ - _____ = _____

My financial net worth is positive or negative?

Once the financial net worth statement is completed, what should be done with it?

When the net worth statement is complete, study it to see what it really says about you and your financial habits. Don't be shocked if your net worth is negative. Many females will have a negative net worth because, as indicated in the statistical facts about females, we save less, invest less, and earn less than males. A negative balance does not mean the end of financial success. Use this information to help you get control and maintain control of your finances.

10 questions for females to ask themselves about their completed financial net worth statement.

1. What is my financial net worth?
2. What is my debt total?
3. How much equity do I have in my home?
4. How much have I saved for retirement?
5. How much have I saved for education or other financial goals?
6. What assets do I need to increase?
7. Which liabilities do I need to decrease?
8. What two things please me about my completed net worth statement?
9. Overall, at this point in my life am I satisfied with my financial net worth?
10. Will I set a goal to increase my financial net worth next year? If so, by how much _____%?

Example: A person should set a goal to increase their financial net worth 3%-5% each year.

Current financial net worth	**$50,000.00**
Increase net worth by 3%	**X .03**
Amount needed to increase	**$ 1,500.00**

$1500 + $50.000 = $51,500 (next year's goal)

 ## Action

Complete a financial net worth statement for your family.

C ongratulations, you now know where you are financially and can start planning where you want to go.

Chapter Three
Plan Your Spending

Are you one of the people that get frustrated because there is always more month that money? Statistics indicate that over 50% of the working population live paycheck to paycheck. You can make a money difference with a spending plan. In most cases lack of money results from lack of planning and understanding. To make your money work, you must learn to plan your spending and understand your expenses.

What are fixed and flexible expenses?

Fixed expenses are those expenses you cannot change. Housing, vehicle payments, and child care are fixed expenses. Fixed expenses are the same each month.

Flexible expenses are those expenses you can control. Food, entertainment, and clothing are flexible. Although, these things are needed, you decide how much you spend on them each month.

Should you plan your spending if you know you have only enough money to pay for the necessities?

Yes, all income and expenses should be planned. Planning will help you get a clear picture of your money and where it is going. It will also help you to see possible areas to decrease spending.

Does planning your spending mean you have to put yourself on a budget?

Yes, planning your spending or developing a spending plan is a more positive way to look at budgeting. Many people are more receptive to the term spending plan because they see it as a plan to assist them in using their money to get things needed and wanted.

What percentage of income and expenses should be planned?

All income should be used to develop a spending plan. A good spending plan will allow you to pay expenses, save, and plan for the future.

What if my spending plan does not work?

A spending plan should be designed to meet the needs of the individual or family. It can and should be changed as often as necessary to make it work. A good spending plan will require you to keep up with your spending for at least one month to determine how much you spend on food, transportation, clothing, and other areas.

Are there any community agencies or organization that will help me develop a spending plan?

Yes, there are many community agencies that will assist you in developing a spending plan. Agencies such as your state Extension Service (number can be found in your local phone book) or the National Foundation for Credit Counseling 1-800-388-2227 are great starting places. Your local bank may also provide assistance in helping you plan your spending. Call and ask about the financial services provided and the cost. Be careful about agencies that charge fees. Make sure you understand what you are paying for and what they ask you to sign.

Should all families have a spending plan?
Yes, it is a good idea for all families with income and expenses to have a spending plan. There is no "one spending plan fits all." Families have different incomes, goals, values, and expenses.

Once a spending plan is developed should it ever be changed?
Yes, a spending plan will need to be changed periodically. Some reasons to change your spending plan: income may increase or decrease; expenses may increase or decrease; needs and desires change; and financial goals change.

Is a spending plan difficult to develop and how do you get started?
No, a spending plan is not difficult to develop. However, a good and reliable plan will require listing all spending for at least one month. This list will make you aware of where your money goes. Once you have tracked expenses you can establish expense categories to cover your spending. Most spending plans will have the following categories: housing, food, utilities, transportation, contributions, personal care, savings, and miscellaneous.

If spending plans are so good, why do people fail to use them or say they don't work?

The number one reason many people fail to use a spending plan or say they do not work is because they have not developed the correct type of spending plan for themselves and their family. A spending plan developed with specific goals in mind, and one that includes all household income and expenses, will work.

What if your income will not cover all of your expenses?

Your spending plan will quickly make you aware of specific problems with your income and expenses. Once problems are identified, you will have to come up with creative ways to resolve the problems. In many cases the problem will require increasing income or decreasing expenses.

➥ **3 ways to increase your income**
   work a second part-time job
   if possible, change tax withholdings
   encourage teens to get part-time jobs (mowing lawns, child care, house cleaning)

➥ **3 ways to decrease your debt**
   avoid using credit
   make more than the minimum payment
   pay off consumer credit accounts

Develop a spending plan for your family. Remember, it should include all income and all expenses.

Family Spending Plan

Monthly Income

Job income . . . . _____

Interest or dividend income . . . . _____

Child support . . . . _____

Alimony . . . . _____

Other . . . . _____

   I. Total of all monthly income . . . . _____

Monthly Expenses

Regular Savings (pay yourself) . . . . _____

Special Savings (goal you're saving for) . . . . _____

   2. Total monthly savings . . . . _____

Housing Expenses

Rent/mortgage . . . . _____

Electric . . . . _____

Gas . . . . _____

Water . . . . _____

Garbage . . . . _____

Telephone . . . . _____

Cable . . . . _____

   3. Total housing expenses . . . . _____

Food Expenses

Food at home . . . . _____

Food away from home . . . . _____

   4. Total food expenses . . . . _____

Consumer Debt

Credit card payments . . . . _____

Loans (furniture, school, finance co.) . . . . _____

Other payments . . . . _____

   5. Total consumer debt . . . . _____

Transportation

Vehicle payments (add all vehicle payments)) . . . . _____

Gas . . . . _____

Maintenance . . . . _____

License . . . . _____

Car phone/Beeper . . . . _____

Other . . . . _____

   6. Total transportation expenses . . . . _____

Clothing
Purchases (clothing & shoes) .... _____
Cleaning .... _____
Other .... _____
    7. Total clothing expenses .... _____

Insurance
Home owners/Renters .... _____
Health/Life .... _____
Vehicle .... _____
Other .... _____
    8. Total insurance expenses .... _____

Education
Tuition .... _____
Books/Magazines .... _____
Other .... _____
    9. Total education expenses .... _____

Contributions/Dues
Church .... _____
Employment / Professional/Social Dues .... _____
    10. Total contributions & dues .... _____

Personal care
Hair Care .... _____
Health club .... _____
Nails & Pedicures .... _____
Body massages .... _____
Other .... _____
    11. Total personal care .... _____

Miscellaneous expenses
Pets .... _____
Hobbies .... _____
Vacations .... _____
Gifts .... _____
Other .... _____
    12. Total Miscellaneous expenses .... _____

    13. Total Expenses (add lines 2-12) .... _____

Subtract total on **line 13** from total on **line 1** for your discretionary income*
_____ - _____ = _____

*Discretionary income is any money left over after all living expenses and bills are paid. Discretionary income allows you to buy the extra things you want. Discretionary income can also be saved and allowed to grow in order to buy more expensive needs and wants.

If you do not have any discretionary income or if your expenses are more than your income make a list of things you are willing to change.

Spending plan changes
1.
2.
3.
4.
5.

Is national information available on family spending?

Yes, each year The Bureau of Labor provides national data on what percentage of the before tax family income is spent in different categories. The most recent information is provided below.

- Housing 31%
- Utilities 7%
- Food 14%
- Clothing 5%
- Health Care 5%
- Transportation 19%
- Life Insurance and Pension 11%
- Entertainment 5%
- Miscellaneous 3%

How do you calculate the percentage of take-home pay going to each category in a spending plan?

To determine spending percentages divide the total amount spent in each category into your household take-home pay.

If you feel you are spending too much, try these tips to cut spending.

Housing – Purchase housing that fits into your budget. Consider sharing costs with a roommate.

Utilities – Consider plans that allow the same monthly payment.

Food – Plan meals before shopping. Do not shop hungry or with kids. Shop sales, use coupons when available. Shop at grocery stores instead of small convenient stores.

Clothing – Purchase at the end of season. Shop sales, shop consignments and thrift stores. Exchange out-grown clothing with family and friends.

Health care – Take care of your body. Eat properly and exercise regularly. Visit the doctor for regular check ups and avoid emergency room costs.

Transportation – Car pool, walk, or use public transportation when available.

Life insurance – Compare rates. Purchase term insurance instead of whole life.

Daily Spending Habits Can Affect Spending Plans*

A cup of coffee at $1.00 a day	=	$	260.00 a year
A soft drink at 75 cents a day	=	$	195.00 a year
A breakfast biscuit at $1.25 a day	=	$	325.00 a year
Lunch at $5.00 a day	=	$	1,300.00 a year
Cigarettes at $4.00 a pack daily	=	$	1,456.00 a year
Shirt laundered at $1.50 each day	=	$	390.00 a year
Beauty shop at $25.00 a week	=	$	1,300.00 a year
Nail shop at $40.00 a month	=	$	480.00 a year
Gasoline at $25.00 a week	=	$	1,300.00 a year

* Calculations based on 52 weeks in a year. Your personal costs may be higher or lower. Do your calculations and see how they impact your spending.

Change a habit and invest what you save.

Stop smoking - invest $100 monthly for 10 years. Receive a 5% return on money invested. Results = $15,528.23.

Action

1. Determine how much of your take-home income goes to housing and food. How does your spending in these areas compare to the national averages on page 21?

    Example: If your monthly income is $1,000.00 and you spend $180.00 per month on food your percentage is 18%. Divide what you spend by your monthly income:

$$\$180.00 \div \$1,000.00 = 18\%$$

National average for food spending is 14%. If you are over the national average, you may want to check what you are buying, where you are shopping and when you are shopping. You may also want to plan meals before shopping.

Calculate your percentages:

Housing

Food

Other

2. Calculate how much your spending habits cost each year. Use the daily cost to determine the weekly cost. Multiply the weekly cost by 52 to get a yearly cost.

Calculate your spending:
A. Chips from snack machine

.75 chips	$ 3.75 weekly
x 5 days	x 52 weeks per year
$3.75 weekly	$195.00 a year

B. Soft drinks

C. Beauty shop

D. Other

Your spending plan will take the guessing out of what happened to your money.

Chapter Four
Out Of Debt For Good

Consumer debt keeps growing and growing and growing. Consumers accumulate over a trillion dollars in debt and pay billions in interests each year. High debt contributes to the increase in the number of bankruptcies filed each year. Last year, more than a million individuals and families filed for bankruptcy. Debt is a BIG problem for many females, but BIG dollars for businesses. Each day millions of credit solicitations are sent to consumers. Females must become educated with ways to get out of and stay out of debt.

Did you know:

•   The average person receives a minimum of 7 credit card mail offers each year.

•   The average interest charged to use a credit card is 18.9%. This means, credit users will repay almost nineteen cents for each credit dollar used.

•   The average American household regularly uses 10 different credit cards.

•   The average household has credit card balances of at least $5,000.

•   The average credit card user can only afford to make minimum monthly credit payments.

- Almost half of Americans in debt indicate that it is difficult making monthly minimum payments.

- The average credit user pays over $1,000 each year in non-deductible tax interest.

Should a person totally avoid using credit?

No. Most people cannot afford to live without using some form of credit. Purchasing a home, renting an apartment, buying a car, using telephone and utility services are all forms of credit. Credit means using a product or service while paying for it. Using credit is a good way to establish a financial reputation. However, when using credit be sure to make payments on time and avoid using more credit than you can afford.

Are there good and bad uses of credit?

Yes. There are good and bad uses of credit. Take the quiz below to see if you can identify some of them.

Credit Quiz

Check each item that is a good use of credit

___1. To purchase a home
___2. To co-sign with a friend who has bad credit
___3. To purchase reliable transportation
___4. To pay for vehicle repairs
___5. To finance an education
___6. To make a "once in a lifetime" investment
___7. To donate to others
___8. To have "pocket money"
___9. To go on a spur of the moment exotic vacation
_10. To start the business of your dreams

Credit Quiz Answers
Good credit uses –

#1 Purchasing a home. Most families cannot afford to pay cash for a home. Mortgage credit is an excellent way to establish a good reputation by making mortgage payments on time each month.

#3 Purchase reliable transportation. Reliable transportation does not have to be a new and expensive vehicle. Consider saving and paying cash for a reliable used vehicle. If you must finance, shop around and compare interest rates at banks, credit unions and other financing sources. Your goal is to get the best rate for your money.

#4 Vehicle repairs. Costly vehicle repairs can require the use of credit. However, if using credit for repairs is your only option, be sure to make payments on time. Consider paying more than the minimum monthly payment to decrease the amount of interest you pay and the length of time you will have to pay.

#5 Finance an education. An education can increase your net worth by making you more marketable and preparing you to earn a higher income. Many institutions will finance an education until a degree program is completed. Once payments are due, make them on time or work with the lending agency to reschedule due date and amount of payments. Failure to pay education loans can result in federal taxes being withheld or pay check garnished.

#10 Finance a business. It is good to use credit to finance a business only after you have done research and know that there is a market for the business. Using credit to finance a business that is not needed will only guarantee more debt.

Bad credit uses –
#2 Co-sign with a friend. Co-signing is agreeing to assume debt if the person you are signing with fails to pay. Instead of co-signing it may be wiser to work with the person to rebuild their credit. A first step to take when working with a person to rebuild credit is to help them develop a spending plan. The next step is encouraging them to save until they have enough money to make a down payment or to pay with cash.

#6 Make an investment. Investments are risky. It is not wise to go in debt to risk money. Also, be very hesitant to invest in opportunities that are "too good to be true."

#7 Donate to others. Getting in debt by donating to others is not a wise decision. If donating to a cause is important to you, try saving or cutting expenses such as eating out or shopping.

#8 Pocket money. It is never a good idea to use credit for cash advances to put money in your pocket. Cash advances are very expensive. Financial institutions usually charge much higher interest on cash advances than on regular purchases. Consider a yard sale to get rid of unwanted items to make extra money. As a last resort, seek small or short-term loans from friends or family members. To keep family and friend loans on a business level, draw up a simple contract outlining repayment details. Both parties should sign the contract. Payments should be followed through until the debt is repaid.

#9 Spur of the moment vacation. Vacations should be planned. Flying off to "a good deal" vacation can end up being an expensive nightmare. Never give your credit card number to callers offering unbelievable vacation opportunities. Check to see if the company making you an offer is valid by calling the State Attorney General's office or the Better Business Bureau.

Are there specific signs to let a person know they are heading for financial trouble?
Yes, there are several early financial warning signs.

- Screening phone calls and refusing to open mail from creditors. Although, most creditors do not turn accounts over for collection agencies until they are several months late, letters are sent and phone calls are made to remind you that a payment is late.

- Regularly using more than 2 credit cards and skipping or only making minimum payments. Minimum payments increase the time it takes to get out of debt and increase the cost of the item because interest is added.

- More than 20% of monthly take-home income after housing expenses goes to credit debt.

Determine credit debt load by finding out how much monthly take-home income goes to creditors.

Monthly income	$2,000.00
Minus Rent	- $ 600.00
Remaining monthly income	$1,400.00

20% of $1,400 = $280; $280 is the most you should use to repay debt.

If you are paying more than 20% of your remaining income to creditors, you are headed for financial trouble. You must increase your income or think of ways to decrease credit obligations to avoid this danger.

- Paying late fees for housing, utilities, car payments, or credit cards.

- Late fee charges have increased in the past few years. Most credit card companies charge $29 for a late fee. Other companies assess a specific dollar amount or a percentage of the outstanding balance. Paying late fees is giving away your money.

- Receiving disconnect notices or having cable, telephone, or utilities disconnected. Disconnects usually carry costly reconnect charges. If you cannot make a payment on time, call and try to work out an arrangement to avoid disconnect and reconnect charges.

- Bouncing checks and regularly paying overdraft charges. Banks and credit unions make a lot of money from charges on bounced checks and overdraft charges. Keep your check book balanced and do not write checks if you know you do not have the money in your account. Also, never post-date checks sent to creditors.

- Skipping monthly credit payments. It is difficult trying to play catch up on skipped credit payments. If there is no possible way to make a credit payment, call creditors immediately and discuss your situation with them.

- Using money in savings to pay rent, car note, or buy groceries.

- Pawning jewelry to pay regular living expenses.

- Cashing savings bonds or IRA before maturity to cover expenses. Extremely high financial penalties are charged for cashing certain investments before they mature. Taxes will also have to be paid. Once penalties and taxes are paid, almost half of the money you've saved is lost.

- Having no money left to save. Get in the habit of paying yourself first. Make sure there is a saving category in your spending plan and treat it as you would any other bill.

- Withdrawing money put in savings before the next pay day.

What should a person do if they cannot afford to pay their bills?

As soon as you realize you are not going to be able to pay creditors, contact them immediately. Explain why you are unable to pay and ask for their help. If special payment plans are made, follow through on the agreement. Do not agree to any plan for which you will be unable to comply.

If a minimum payment cannot be paid, should the payment be skipped or should a smaller payment be sent?

It is always better to make some payment than no payment at all. If, however, you are not able to make a full payment, contact creditors, explain your situation, and make them aware of the payment amount you are sending.

If money is limited how do you determine which bills to pay first?

It is important to always cover personal financial obligations. However, there may be times that financial hardships occur and you are uncertain who to pay first. Consider the following guidelines:

1st priority –

    Cover living necessities-housing, utilities and food.

2nd priority –

    Cover expenses that may cause legal or employment problems such as bounced checks.

3rd priority –
    Cover expenses with creditors in which you have secured properties such as your automobile.
4th priority –
    Cover expenses that may cause legal actions such as: credit cards, medical or furniture bills.

Is bankruptcy the best way to start over financially?

No. Bankruptcy can have long-term consequences and should only be considered if you are unemployed and have no other options. Also, anyone considering bankruptcy should become educated on the difference between Chapter 7 and Chapter 13.

What is the difference between a Chapter 7 and a Chapter 13 Bankruptcy?

Chapter 13 is an approved debt repayment plan. The plan allows a person to repay all or a percentage of the outstanding debt over a three to five year period. Payments are made to a court appointed trustee who sends payments directly to creditors. Chapter 13 will remain on the credit report for 7 years.

Chapter 7 is referred to as straight bankruptcy. It allows the dismissal of all debt obligations except child support, student loans, federal and state taxes and alimony. Filers are allowed to keep a specified amount of personal properties and the remainder are sold. Monies from the sale of properties are shared between creditors. Chapter 7 bankruptcy remains on a credit report for 10 years.

Is bankruptcy automatically removed after 7 or 13 years?

No. Bankruptcy trustees work hard to make sure timely information is sent to credit reporting agencies after filers are dismissed, but this is not always the case. Filers must be prepared to check their credit report and make reporting agencies aware of their dismissal.

What is a credit report?

A credit report is a document used to make creditors aware of a potential customer's credit history. It is very difficult to hide a negative financial background. Your credit report will tell creditors if you pay bills on time, how many creditors you have, how much debt you are in, if you are employed and if you have ever filed for bankruptcy.

Can I request a copy of my spouse's credit report?

No. You can request a joint credit report for you and your spouse or a personal copy of your own credit report, but you cannot request a personal copy of your spouse's report without his permission.

Is your credit report made available to anyone that wants to see it?

No, credit reports are confidential. However, they are made available when you request approval for:

- Housing
- Credit
- Life insurance
- Employment paying over $20,000 a year

Does everyone in debt have a credit report?

Yes. Most people in debt have credit reports. However, females may not have a credit report if all credit accounts are in their husband's name. It is important that females establish a credit history to allow them to qualify for credit if needed. Married females can request household payments be reported in both husband's and wife's names.

How can females establish credit in their name?

Females can establish a credit history by opening a small account in a department store or by getting a small loan at a bank or credit union and making regular timely payments.

When should a person request a copy of their credit report?

A person should check their credit report at least once a year or before purchasing a major item such as a vehicle or house. The purpose of viewing before making a purchase it to make sure there is no incorrect information on the report. If there is incorrect information you must request an audit of the information in writing from the company supplying the report. The company has up to 30 days to correct information or remove it from your report. There is no cost to correct information. However, there is usually a small cost to receive a copy of your credit report, unless you were denied credit, then it is free.

How do you request a copy of a credit report?

Credit reports can be requested from one of three different reporting agencies.

Equifax - 1-800-685-1111
P.O. Box 105873
Atlanta, GA 30348
www.equifax.com

Experian - 1-888-397-3742
P.O. Box 2104
Allen, TX 75013
www.experian.com

Trans Union Corporation - 1-800-916-8800
P.O. Box 390
Springfield, PA 19064
www.transunion.com

What is a FICO Score?

A FICO score is the score that results when the information on your credit report is translated into a number. A FICO score can range from 300 to 850. An average score is around 620. The higher the FICO score the lower the interest rate offered by creditors. FICO Scores can be purchased online at www.myfico.com.

How often can debt payments be missed before it shows up on your credit report?

Credit information is reported to the credit bureau every 30 days. Each time a debt payment is 30 days late it will show up on your credit report. Late payments are indicated by a number. Credit report numbers range from 1-9. One through 8 indicate number of late days and 9 indicates a repossession has taken place.

Example:

1 - payments made on time
2 - payment is 30 days late
3 - payment is 60 days late
4 - payment is 90 days late

How long does information remain on a credit report?

Regular information remains on a credit report for seven years. If a bankruptcy has been taken, information will remain on the credit report for up to ten years.

Can a lawyer or credit repair company remove bad information from credit reports?

No. Federal laws prohibit any true information from being removed from a credit report before a specified time frame, seven years unless a bankruptcy has occurred.

If I am committed to getting out of debt, where do I start?

Use the following six steps to get started.

Six steps to debt freedom

Step 1:   Make a personal commitment to be "Debt Free." Nothing will change how you use your money until you are ready for and committed to the change.

Step 2:   Stop using credit. Cut up credit cards or return them to the company with a note requesting the closing of the account. Having credit cards around only tempts you to use them.

Step 3:   Determine your financial net worth and total debt **(see Chapter 2).** Know where you are financially. No goals can be set until you know where you are and where you want to go.

Step 4:   Develop a debt free plan. Determine how long it will take you to pay off your debt. Contact your local Cooperative Extension Service office in the government pages of the telephone directory. Ask if they have PowerPay, a computer debt pay off program. PowerPay is used by many Extension offices across the country. Banks, credit unions, churches or other community non-profit organizations may provide programs or services to assist you in developing a debt payoff plan. Bankcard Holders of America offers a debt reduction program called Debt Zapper, which uses total debt amounts, interest rates, and monthly payments to calculate how long it will take you to get out of debt. There is a small cost for the service. For details write: Bankcard Holders of America, 524 Branch Drive, Salem, VA 24153.

Step 5: Put your debt free plan in action. After you have developed your plan, use it.

Step 6: Evaluate your plan every 3 months. Ask yourself the following questions as you evaluate your plan:
Is my debt decreasing?
Am I feeling better about my financial situation?
What other things can I change to make my financial situation even better?

 **Action**

What actions will you take as a result of reading this chapter. Make an appointment with yourself and mark it on your calendar.

Actions   **When (date)**

___Check credit report   _____

___Calculate personal/family debt load   _____

___Make a commitment to get out of debt   _____

___Develop a debt free plan   _____

___Share information with family/friend   _____

___Other (list)_____   _____

Take charge of your financial life so that you will be able to get more out of life than debt.

Chapter Five
Survive Financially After A Death Or Divorce

Current statistics indicate that 90% of females can expect to be alone at some point in their life. Death and divorce are two leading causes of females being alone. Although death and divorce are realities, they are both devastating experiences and often leave females unprepared to assume financial responsibilities.

Death
This section will focus on some of the issues females will need to address as they go through the death of a spouse. The information provided should not replace professional legal advice in the state in which the female lives. Never guess or pretend you understand answers that may be given to questions you have. Ask and re-ask questions until you are confident that you have enough information to make the best decision for you and your family.

If a husband dies without a Will, do all his assets automatically go to his widow?
No. Very few states will award a widow all of her spouse's assets. Most states allows the widow one-third to one half of the assets. Children, parents, or siblings receive the other percentage. Be sure to seek legal advice in your state if this is a concern.

Are Wills and Estate Plans the same thing?
No. A Will is only one part of an Estate Plan. An Estate Plan is a detailed document. It protects financial resources from taxes and provides directions on how to distribute personal property and income upon a person's death. A lawyer specializing in estate planning should be used to help you develop an Estate Plan. The cost will vary depending on detail. Banks, family members, friends or the Bar Association can help you locate an estate planning lawyer.

What does probate mean?
Probate is the process by which the probate court oversees the paying of debts, taxes, and other expenses as well as transferring property left to beneficiaries after a death.

Is probating a Will expensive and how long does it take?
Yes. Probating can be expensive. The probate cost usually depends on the amount of the estate. Costs can range from 5% to 25% or more of the total estate. Probating may take a few months to a few years. The length of time depends on the amount of property, people and problems involved in the process.

Are safe deposit boxes really sealed upon death and, if so, why?
Yes. Most states require the sealing of a safe deposit box until the contents are inspected by tax authorities to

verify that everything that is supposed to be in the box is there.

Can a husband write a Will to disinherit his wife?

No. State laws do not allow legally married couples to disinherit the other. A Will can, however, prevent the surviving spouse from receiving more assets than what the law requires.

How do I find a good lawyer?

The best way to locate a good lawyer is by word of mouth recommendation from someone you trust. If that is not an option, contact the bar association in your town. Explain the type of service you need and ask them to give you several names of lawyers who can provide the service. Telephone the lawyers and schedule a consultation. Most lawyers will extend a free consultation to potential new clients.

What important papers or documents are needed to take care of business after a spouse's death?

Many important papers will be necessary as you go through the process of burying and collecting benefits after a spouse's death. These documents should be organized in your family files and in a place that is easily accessible.

Important Papers
Copy of spouse's Will
Insurance policies
Donor cards
Birth certificate
Social security card
Marriage license
Recent income tax returns
Military papers
Employment benefit papers
Retirement benefit papers

Should property titles and ownership be changed after a spouse's death?

Yes. Failure to change property titles and ownership from your spouse's name after his death could cause problems in the future. Some items you want to be sure to change are:

Your Will
Credit accounts
Safe deposit box
Investments
Insurance policies
Bank accounts
Home Mortgage
Vehicle registrations

How do you know if you qualify for spousal benefits, and how do you apply for them?

Common benefits spouses usually apply for are:

Social Security Benefits – Contact the social security office. They may provide a one time death benefit and can be helpful if you qualify for monthly social security benefits. You may also qualify for social security benefits if you are an ex-spouse and meet social security's qualifications.

Insurance Benefits – Contact the policy holder. Don't forget to check with bank and credit unions. Your spouse may have signed up for one of the policies provided by financial institutions at low or no cost.

Military Benefits – If spouse is currently in the military or served in the military and was honorably discharged, you could qualify for benefits. Contact the Veteran's Administration

Employee Benefits – Contact current and former employers. Former employers may have provided pensions or other benefits that were not taken when the employee left.

What is the best way to receive cash benefits from spouse's life insurance?

Only the family involved can make the decision about what is best for them when it involves receiving life insurance. There are three basic ways life insurance benefits can be received.

One-time lump sum payment – The entire face value of the insurance is paid in one lump sum.

Installment payments – Insurance company divides the value of the insurance funds in equal fixed amounts and distributes them at specified times until funds are depleted.

Annuities – The insurance company make monthly payments in a specified amount for a specified time frame.

Should insurance benefits be invested immediately?

No. It is recommended that life insurance cash benefits be placed in a short-term low risk investment such as a Certificate of Deposit or Money-Market for at least three to six months. This time frame gives the beneficiary time to evaluate investment options and think through important financial needs.

What financial decisions should be considered with life insurance cash benefits?

The following list is only a suggestion of the things to consider. Your family, lawyer, or financial planner can assist with a more complete and personalized list of other things to consider:

Child's education
A retirement plan for yourself
Your education
Health care coverage
Debt obligations

Divorce

Currently, one out of two marriages end in divorce. Research indicates that women, especially those with children, are likely to experience a decrease in financial well-being after a divorce. If you are considering divorce or are going through a divorce, remember that you will need to survive financially after the divorce. A good financial reputation is a must for females after a divorce. Therefore, as you go through the divorce don't lose sight on the finances. Make sure you get sound legal advice and do not rely on hearsay information.

Can females expect financial support after a divorce?

No. Females can no longer expect that they will automatically be awarded the children, child support, or alimony in a divorce settlement. More fathers are filing for sole custody or joint custody and are sharing in the cost to raise children after a divorce.

What can I do if I am awarded child support, but my ex-spouse will not pay it?

Collecting child-support is a concern for many divorced women. If you have been awarded child-support and are not receiving it, contact your local Department of Human Services or the Child Support Division of the local court and report it. They will assist you in getting the necessary paperwork in place to start the collection process.

There are also many private organizations listed in the yellow pages of the telephone directory that help women collect child-support. You may contact them or call the Association for Children for Enforcement of Support (ACES) at 1-800-537-7072. ACES is a child-support educational organization. They will work with you personally to collect child-support or put you in touch with a local ACES chapter.

What determines if a female is awarded alimony?

Permanent alimony is usually awarded only when a spouse has mental or physical disabilities and cannot take care of themselves. Temporary alimony may be awarded for a specified time to allow females to become educated and marketable in the job world.

Can females be required to pay alimony?

Yes. Females can be required to pay alimony if their income is more than their spouse's and if he is awarded custody or joint custody of the children. If this is a concern, it is important that legal counsel be consulted.

If funds are low, is it okay to stop making payments until the divorce is final?

No. Bills must be paid monthly throughout the divorce process. Any skipped or late payments will show up on your credit report and will remain there for up to seven years. Late payments can make it difficult for future credit.

How should joint credit accounts listed in both names be treated after a divorce?

Joint accounts should be closed and reopened as single accounts. Do not depend on creditors to take your word for who is responsible for paying the bill. If one party refuses to pay, creditors will seek payment from the other spouse on the account.

How do you close joint accounts?

Call creditors to make them aware that you are sending a letter to close the account. Request that a notation of your call be made on the account file. Then, write a letter indicating that you are going through a divorce and would like to have the joint account closed and reopened as a separate account. Creditors are likely to request a new credit application to be sure that you can afford future payment obligations.

If my credit is damaged in the divorce process, will a letter from my lawyer to all creditors be enough to help me establish or re-establish credit in my name?

No. A letter from your lawyer cannot help with your credit reputation. Your credit report and how you handled credit in the past will always be your most important credit building tool.

Will creditors remove joint account information from credit reports after a divorce?

No. Creditors will not automatically remove information on joint accounts after a divorce. Account information will continue to be reported as joint until those accounts are closed or changed.

How helpful are credit repair companies in repairing a damaged credit report after a divorce?

Not very helpful. Credit repair companies charge large fees and make promises. In all honesty, they cannot do anything to your credit report that you cannot do for yourself. True information must remain on your credit report seven to ten years.

What is a divorce mediator, and are there any advantages to using one?

A divorce mediator is a person who works with divorcing couples to help them determine property settlements and custody arrangements when children are involved. The advantage of using a divorce mediator is that they are usually able to work with couples to come to agreements in a more timely manner and therefore decrease time and costs associated with a divorce. Lawyers often recommend divorce mediators or they can be located by using a telephone directory.

Are there times when it is to your advantage to remain married?

Yes. Ten years of marriage entitles you to receive social security benefits from an ex-spouse's earnings. So, if you are approaching a ten year marriage you may want to consider prolonging the divorce process. Social security is a benefit to you as long as you do not remarry. Your receiving social security does not impact your ex-spouse's social security even if he remarries.

Be Prepared for the unexpected - Organize your important papers.

Whether you are faced with a death or divorce you must be able to quickly locate important papers to verify, document or change information. Use the following suggestions to organize your important papers.

Important papers should be kept in four places:

1. Wallet or billfold
2. Home files
3. Vehicle
4. Safe deposit box

Suggested papers to keep in wallet or billfold:

- License
- Donor card
- Medical card
- Health insurance card

Suggested papers to keep in vehicle:
- Copy of vehicle registration
- Copy of vehicle insurance

Suggested papers to keep in safe deposit box
- Original birth certificate
- Original marriage certificate
- Original death certificate
- Original insurance policies
- Property deeds & titles
- Military separation papers
- Investment certificates
- Copy of will
- List of household valuable contents (video contents)
- Adoption papers

Suggested papers for home files:
- List of credit card accounts and telephone numbers
- Updated copy of net worth statement
- Current year of credit account canceled checks
- Passport
- Copy of birth certificates
- Copy of marriage certificates
- Copy of will
- Original title of vehicle
- Tax return (last 3 to 5 years)
- Product warranties
- Employment papers
- Education papers
- Copy of insurance policies

The lists above are only suggestions. You and your family should make the final decisions on what papers to keep in which files.

How do you determine if you should keep certain papers?

You cannot keep all of the papers you receive. The best way to determine if papers should be kept is to ask yourself the following question: "If I had to replace this document, how difficult would it be?" If the item would be very difficult or impossible to replace it should be kept. If the item could easily be replaced by making a phone call, it's probably okay to trash it.

Be Sure to Keep These Papers

Tax returns & receipts	up to 7 years
Credit account statements	1 year
Bank statements	up to 10 years
Property titles & deeds	until property is sold
Investment certificates	until sold
Utility & telephone bills	trash monthly*
Loan agreements	indefinitely
Birth & Death certificates	indefinitely
Education Records	indefinitely
Vehicle Titles	until vehicle is sold

*company will supply a summary if needed

 **Action**

If you or someone in your family needed to locate your important papers would they be able to? If not, schedule time to organize your important papers.

Do you have the correct papers in the correct files? Use the suggestion lists in the chapter to help you decide how and where to file your important papers.

Make a list of the files you will organize. Have family members to assist in this task, it will make them aware of where you keep the family important papers.

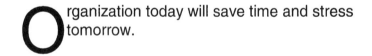

O rganization today will save time and stress tomorrow.

Chapter Six
Communicate About Your Money

Money is the number one reason for arguments in the home. It is also cited as the number one reason for over 90% of marriages in America ending in divorce. Every female can share an experience about money that has made them happy, sad, depressed, excited, or fearful. It is amazing how one thing can impact so many different emotions, but money can.

The way we use money reflects our feelings about money. No two people will have the same feelings about money nor will they have the same money values. Failure to understand the money values of others in the family will cause family conflict. Therefore, it is important to discuss how you feel about money and how you think it should be used.

Should money decisions be left up to the person making the money in the household?

No. Decisions made about how to spend household money should involve everyone in the household. This is especially true if you want all household members to assist with reaching a household financial goal. Studies show that people are more committed to reaching goals if they help set the goals.

What are family financial goals and why should they be discussed?

Family financial goals serve as a road map to help families get what they want financially. Financial goals also outline exactly what you want, when you want to have it, and how you go about getting it.

Example:
Financial Goal should include what, when and how much?

Want to save $500 for a trip to Fun Park in 6 months.
$500 ÷ 6 months = $84.00

To reach goal:
Save $84.00 each month
Save $42.00 every two weeks

Financial experts say, "children should be included in family money discussions and decisions." Is this a good idea?

Yes. Children must learn how to make good money decisions. Allowing them an opportunity to share in family money discussions and decisions will give them experience in planning, thinking through options, determining costs, negotiating and compromising.

Are most arguments in the home the result of not having enough money to meet family needs?

No. Many family arguments over money are likely to be linked to power, control, and lack of communication about how the money should be spent.

In a married couple household should one person be responsible for managing the money?

No. Both adults in the household should be familiar with all financial resources and obligations. One person may be assigned to the monthly managing because they enjoy the job or they have the best management skills. Periodically, however, couples should jointly share the task to be sure both parties know how the family is doing financially.

What is a good way to discuss money in the household without starting an argument?

Timing is the key to discussing household money issues. When you sense the time is right, ask your spouse if the two of you could set an appointment to discuss family finances and to set financial goals. You may also want to agree upon an agenda for the meeting so that both of you will be prepared. Make sure the agenda is not overbearing. At the end of the meeting make another appointment with each other. Continue the appointments until you are comfortable and knowledgeable of the finances in your household.

When are the best and worst times to discuss money?

Best times:
>　at planned family meetings
>　at agreed upon times
>　while working on a spending plan

Worst times:
>　during a meal
>　immediately after work
>　after a stressful day
>　late at night
>　in front of family or friends
>　during or immediately after paying bills

Is it okay to have separate money accounts if couples cannot agree on how to spend the money they make?

Yes, but only if it is discussed and both parties agree to separate accounts.

Does it make sense to have a joint household account and separate accounts for each spouse?

Yes. Separate accounts will allow couples to keep their personal allowance funds separate from agreed upon joint household funds. Joint household expenses usually include, but are not limited to: rent or mortgage, utilities, phone, auto payments, auto insurance, childcare and food.

Is there a fair way to divide household expenses if one spouse makes more money than the other and if separate money accounts are desired?

Yes. Each spouse can contribute an equal percentage of their take-home income based on household expenses. To determine how much each spouse must contribute, follow the instructions below:

Together make a list of all household expenses (rent, telephone, food, utilities, etc.) and determine how much is spent monthly on these items.

Example: Total monthly household expenses = $2,500.00

Add the total take-home income of both spouses:
$1,500.00
+ $3,000.00
$4,500.00

Divide the household expenses by total take-home income:
$2,500.00
÷ $4,500.00
56%

Each spouse will contribute 56% of their take-home income to a joint household account to cover household expenses.

$1,500.00 $3,000.00
x   56%   x   56%
$ 840.00 $1,680.00

How do you avoid feeling guilty about spending on yourself?

Try to understand why you feel guilty about spending. Is it because you are afraid of comments that may be made about the purchase, or is it because you feel you do not have the money? Ask all family members, including yourself, to make a list of things you need or would like to have. Include on the list a date and approximate cost of each item. Share the lists at a family meeting. Ask if there are any concerns about your list. If there are no concerns start working on a plan to accumulate the items on the list. If there are concerns, address them up front. You may also want to discuss making an allowance available to all family members. This will give each person an opportunity to have money to do some of the things they would like to do without worrying or feeling guilty.

🔍 Action

- When was the last time your family discussed finances?
- If something happened to you or your spouse would the other spouse (or children) know how to manage the family finances? If not, schedule a family meeting to discuss finances.
- Do you know how much your family is worth in dollars and cents? If not, schedule an appointment and together develop a family net worth statement.
- Do you have any written family financial goals? If not, schedule an appointment with each other to discuss goals you would like to achieve. Write them down and post them where you can see them.

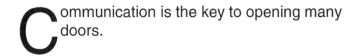

Communication is the key to opening many doors.

Chapter Seven
Children And Money

Have you ever stopped to think how much money children have available to spend? According to Teenage Research Unlimited, teens 12-19 years of age spend over 170 billion dollars annually. Each year the amount of money children spend continues to grow. Financial experts predict that if we do not teach children good money management skills, we will continue to see high bankruptcy rates. In a study to better understand who is teaching children about money, mothers (43%) were cited as the person most responsible for teaching children about money. Children as young as 3 years old understand that money is used to buy the things they want. Therefore, teaching children about money can and should start early in life.

Should children receive allowances?
Yes. Allowances give children the opportunity to learn how to manage money. It also teaches them responsibility.

At what age should children receive an allowance?
Children as young as 3 years olds can be given a small allowance and taught to save some of it in a piggy bank, put some in church, and spend some on a special treat.

How much of an allowance should a child receive?

Parents should decide how much they can afford and what they expect children to do with their allowance before they decide on a specific amount. They will also have to decide if the allowance will be given weekly, bi-weekly or monthly. Their decision should be based on household income, expenses, and the needs of children. Allowance should be enough to cover expected expenses and to save. Some parents set a specific dollar amount based on household chores while others determine the amount based on a child's age (a ten year old will receive $10). As you determine the amount to give, keep in mind that giving too much can be as bad as not giving enough.

Should an allowance be tied to household chores?

No. An allowance is to teach money skills and financial responsibilities. Children should be made to understand that as a family member certain responsibilities, such as keeping their personal bedroom and bathroom clean, is expected. Other chores such as dusting, cleaning windows, cutting grass, polishing silver and vacuuming may be ways to earn extra money above their regular allowance.

How often should allowances be given?

Most parents choose to give allowances in conjunction to when they get paid. However, young children need to learn how to manage money for short periods of time before being expected to keep it for 2-4 weeks. Try giving smaller allowances weekly, then graduate to every 2 weeks as management skills develop. Teens are usually prepared to handle more money for longer periods of time. Just be sure they understand, "when their allowance is gone, it's gone."

Under what conditions should a parent deny a child their allowance?

Allowances should be continued once started, unless family financial situations prevent them. Remember, an allowance is given to teach financial skills and responsibilities, and these practices should be ongoing.

Should parents put stipulations on the child's use of the allowance?

Parents should encourage children to divide their allowance in categories. Suggested categories could include: saving for the future (a car or summer camp), saving for an up-coming event (homecoming dance or friend's birthday gift), spending on something they want immediately (going to the movies). You may also use an allowance to teach church tithing (one dime out of every dollar is set aside to put in church).

If a child spends all of their allowance should parents give additional money?

No. Children should understand that they need to manage their allowance to cover activities in which they want to participate. Lack of planning and managing their money will result in missed opportunities. It will not take children long to realize the importance of saving if they have to miss one or two events. This experience will also teach them the value of preparing for the future rather than experiencing immediate gratification. There may be times that unforeseen situations will arise that may require you to give additional money. Under these circumstances consider having the child write a simple loan agreement and present it to you.

The agreement should include how much they want to borrow and the specifics on how you will be repaid. The loan agreement should be dated and signed by both you and your child.

At what age should a child open a bank account?

Most banks and credit unions do not have an age requirement for children to open a savings account. The younger they are when you open it the more their money will grow. Children as young as 3 years old can be exposed to taking their money to the bank. Many banks and credit unions have special kid clubs and give gifts to young children who open an account. Learning to manage a checking account is a great experience for teens. Once they learn to manage a checking account, consider putting enough money in it allow them to write the check each month for their braces or personal products.

At what age should children know about family household income and expenses?

Children should be taught the basics of managing money as soon as they start asking for money to make purchases. An allowance is an excellent way to teach the basics of saving and planning purchases. Other more detailed family financial issues should be shared with a child when they are mature enough to understand that family income is a personal topic and should not be discussed outside the family. When you are comfortable that your child has reached that level, allow them to assist with developing the household spending plan, food shopping with a budget and writing checks that you sign.

Are there any children's books or web sites to help parents teach children about money?

Yes. The following children's books are about money. Kids LOVE them.

The Bernstein Bears & Mama's New Job
The Bernstein Bears' Trouble with Money
A Bargain for Frances
Alexander, Who Used to be Rich Last Sunday
The Purse
Tight Times

Here's one of my favorite web sites. Parents and teachers will love it.

www.unce.unr.edu/Western/SubWebs/MoneyOnTheBookshelf/ChildrensBooksAboutMoney.htm

 Action

- Teach young children 3-5 years old how to recognize coins by name and appearance. They can also be taught to save.
- Teach children 6 and up the value of coins and how to count money. Use coins to teach how many pennies equal a nickel or a dime. How many nickels equal a quarter, and so on.
- Teach children 7 and up how to count money after making a purchase to see if they received the correct change. Start with small single purchases and build on the concept.
- Teach children 8 and up how to develop a simple spending plan using their allowance as income. Have them write down all expenses and subtract this amount from their income (allowance). Make sure they receive an adequate allowance to allow them to manage church dues, savings, and personal spending money. As the child gets older and the allowance is increased, the spending plan should be more detailed.
- Teach teens how to manage a checking account, shop and compare prices for car insurance and understand investing by reading the stock pages in the newspaper.

M oney smart children grow up to be money smart adults.

Chapter Eight
I Can't Save And Forget Investing

Americans save less than any other developed country in the world. Although, today more people are saving than in the past, most American families save less than ten percent of their annual salary. This level of saving is not likely to support the retirement years or cover other costly long-term goals.

Many financial experts say that the most important step to investing is getting started. My suggestion to all females is to prepare for investing. Remember investing serves in assisting you with reaching future goals. Once you start, you do not want to interrupt the process.

How often should one save?
Savings should be a regular commitment and done each payday.

Is there a recommended amount to save, or should bills be paid and then savings considered?
Yes, there is a recommended amount of money to save. It is recommended that 10% of gross income (gross is the total amount of income before taxes and deductions are subtracted) is saved. If one cannot afford 10% of gross, then 10% of net income (net income is the amount of money actually taken home), If one cannot afford 10% of net income try 5%. The

most important thing to consider in saving is to save an agreed upon amount regularly.

When should savings be used?
Only you and your family can set guidelines for using money saved. However, some recommended ways to use savings are:
- To cover unexpected emergencies
- To cover the cost of items for which you were saving

When is saving better than investing?
Saving is a form of investing. Saving is less risky than investing and usually does not have the potential to grow as fast as money invested. It is better to save when:
- Risk must be avoided
- Money must be easily accessible
- Money is being saved to reach short-term goals (less than 5 years)

Invest when:
- Risks can be taken
- Large money growth is needed
- Money is needed to reach long-term goals (5 years or more)
- You have three months of household living expenses saved to cover emergencies.

Where is the best place to save money?
Federally insured financial institutions are the best places to save money. Insured means the institutions will cover up to $100,000 in any account. Most institutions will have FDIC or NCUA signs posted to

indicate that they are insured. If you do not see the signs posted, ask for them.

How do you decide which financial institution to use?

Shop around to determine the one that offers the best interest rates. You should also select one that is conveniently located, has operating hours to match your schedule, and offers services that meet your needs.

How do you prepare to start investing?

Investing requires a long-term commitment. Therefore, before investing, consider having the following things in place:

- Specific written goals. Know what you want to achieve.
- Family insurance coverage. Make sure you and your family are covered in case of emergencies.
- Good credit practices. Be a wise credit user and know what your credit report says about you.
- Savings to cover 3-6 months of expenses.

If income is low where do you get money to save or invest?

Use creative ways to accumulate extra money to save or invest.

- Save coins
- Work overtime
- Create extra job opportunities (baby sitting, word processing, home maintenance)
- Request money for gifts
- Use income tax returns

- Use money saved with coupons or by shopping sales
- Save aluminum cans, glass bottles, or newspapers and sell for recycling
- Have a yard sale

Do you need to hire an investment broker to help you start investing?

No. You do not need an investment broker to start investing. In many instances you can work with a banker, a financial planner with an investment company, an insurance agent, or an accountant to help you start investing.

Is it possible to consider investing with less than $100 a month?

Yes. Many people do not know it is possible to invest $50 or less monthly. Many companies encourage regular investing by having small monthly automatic deductions made from a bank or credit union account. Small amounts invested regularly add up to big dollars over time.

Where is the best place to start investing if you can only afford $50 or less each month?

A Mutual fund is the best place to start investing if you can commit to investing for 5 years or more. Mutual funds may include stocks and bonds. They are relatively safe, professionally managed, and use funds pooled by a group of investors. Mutual funds may be purchased through a banker, financial planner, insurance company, or broker.

Is a Certificate of Deposit (CD) considered investing or saving?

Remember, saving is a form of investing. A certificate of deposit is often referred to as a savings with a higher rate of interest. Unlike some other investments, CDs do not have purchasing fees. They are safe but offer very low rates of return.

If you have a set amount of savings is there anyway to determine how long it will take the money to double in value?

Yes. The rule of 72 is an excellent way to estimate how long it will take your money to double in value. To use this rule you must know when you will need the money or anticipate a specific rate of return on the money being saved. Divide either number into 72 to get your answer.

Example:
Money needed in 9 years
$72 \div 9 = 8\%$ return is needed to double savings in 9 years.

Anticipate 10% rate of return
$72 \div 10\% = 7.2$ years is needed to double savings with a 10% return.

Why should females save more than males?

Females on the average live longer than males and make less than males. Therefore, they are at greater risk of outliving their retirement savings and facing poverty during their retirement years.

Is an automatic deduction savings plan a good idea?

Yes. Automatic deduction is often the best way to develop an on-going monthly saving habit. Savers usually start small and increase as their income increases. Money is less likely to be missed if it is subtracted before bills are paid instead of afterwards.

 **Action**

How do the following questions apply to your financial situation?

1. Do you save each month?   ___Yes ___No
2. Do you have an investment account?   ___Yes ___No
3. List three of your financial goals? Will they require saving or investing?

    Goals _____   Save or Invest?
    A.

    B.

    C.

4. Are you prepared to start investing? If not what changes do you need to make?
5. Develop an action plan to start reaching your saving and investment goals?
6. Which goal will you work on first and when will you get started? Be specific.

Saving a little now will mean a lot later.

Chapter Nine
Get Ready For Retirement

A female friend once asked me, "When should a person really start planning for retirement?" My answer to her without hesitation was, "The first day they start working." Unfortunately many females and males start thinking about and planning for retirement too late. As a result, many have not saved enough money to finance the retirement years and must continue in the work force longer than they would like.

How much should a person plan to save to cover the cost of retirement?

There is no set amount every person should save for retirement. People are different. Therefore, they will have different goals and needs. It is recommended that 60% to 85% of current income is saved for the retirement years. How much will depend on your retirement plans. A current income of $40,00 at 60% equals $24,000 in retirement income. A current income of $40,000 at 85% equals $34,000 in retirement income.

Other than retirement income, what other ideas should one consider when planning for retirement?

Consider what you will do and where will you live? Will you relocate to another state? Will you purchase a smaller home or move into a retirement community? Is there a need for a new vehicle, household furnishings or appliances? How much do you plan to travel? Will you need additional medical coverage or are your medical benefits adequate? Contact American Association of Retired Persons (AARP) 601 E Street, NW Washington, DC 20049 for additional resources to help you plan for retirement.

Should a person really expect their expenses to be lower during retirement?

Yes. Some expenses will be lower during retirement, but others are likely to increase. The list below will assist in identifying areas that may increase or decrease after one retires.

Decrease	Increase
Housing*	Medical expenses
Work clothing	Dental expenses
Work dues	Travel expenses
Taxes	
Retirement savings	
Life insurance	
Work transportation expenses	

*lower if mortgage is paid off

What should determine if you retire or continue to work?

The best determining factors to retire or not to retire are: your health, your retirement benefits, and your ability to financially afford retirement. Unfortunately, many people wait too late to start planning for retirement and discover they cannot afford retirement.

How do you know for how many retirement years to financially plan?

There is no definite way to determine life expectancy after retirement. However, Insurance companies use life expectancy projections to sell life insurance and predict that individuals retiring in good health at age 65 can expect to live 20 years or longer after they retire.

What if you know you cannot afford to save the recommended amount of money for retirement?

Your inability to save the recommended amount for retirement may require you to change some of your retirement plans. It may also mean working longer to increase the amount of income you will have at retirement. Start now and save regularly. Save as much as you can.

Where is the best place to keep my retirement funds?

Retirement funds should be kept in a place that will allow you to receive the highest growth at your most comfortable level of risk. Investments are categorized as low risk, medium risk and high risk. Low risk products include regular savings accounts, certificates of deposit, fixed annuities, and Treasury bills. Medium risk products include some mutual funds, bonds and some stocks. High risk products include certain tax shelters, some bond funds and some stocks. The lower the risk you are willing to assume with your retirement funds the lower the earning potential for your money to grow. The higher the risk, the higher the potential for money to grow.

Should one participate in an employer's retirement plan or locate one outside the company?

Most individuals are much better off participating in a company's retirement plan. Many companies offer 401(k) plans. This plan offers employees an opportunity to save for retirement by investing before tax income. Some companies match retirement funds up to a certain percentage or dollar amount, allowing retirement dollars to grow faster.

If retirement savings are needed to cover family expenses, is it possible to withdraw it?

Yes. It is possible, but you will be penalized. Funds withdrawn before age 59½ are accessed a 10% penalty and will require that income taxes are paid.

Do years of service really affect retirement income?

Yes. Years of service determine what percentage of current income will be received during retirement. 10 years of services 10-15%, 20 years 20-25%, 30 years 30-35%.

A person retiring with a $25,000 income
10 years at 10% = $2,500 retirement annually or $208 monthly
20 years at 20% = $5,000 retirement annually or $416 monthly
30 years at 30% = $7,500 retirement annually or $625 monthly

Does everyone receive social security after they retire?

No. Retired federal employees do not receive social security benefits. Social security is only paid to individuals that meet the required qualifications. To qualify one must have 40 quarter hours, or 10 years, of work experience.

Is it possible to check on social security qualifications before you retire?

Yes. Starting in October 1998 all employed individuals should receive an annual social security statement. If you have not received one contact your local social security office or call 1-800-772-1213 to request a social security application.

What is a ROTH IRA?

A ROTH IRA is an individual retirement plan that taxes investments up front instead of taxing when the investment is withdrawn.

My Social Security will not be adequate to fund my retirement years. If I commit to saving $1,000 each year for ten years how much can I withdraw monthly during retirement?

The amount you are able to withdraw will depend on the rate of return received on the money invested for the future. The example below will allow you to see how much $1,000.000 will grow over time and how much you will be able to withdraw monthly for 10, 20 and 30 years.

$1,000.00 saved each year with an 8% return:

Years Saved	Total Saved with Interest	Monthly Payments 10 years	20 years
10	$ 15,645.00	$ 188.00	$ 128.00
20	$ 49,422.00	$ 592.00	$ 405.00
30	$122,500.00	$1,266.00	$1,022.00

$1,000.00 saved each year with an 10% return:

Years Saved	Total Saved with Interest	Monthly Payments 10 years	20 years
10	$ 17,531.00	$ 228.00	$ 164.00
20	$ 63,002.00	$ 818.00	$ 590.00
30	$180,943.00	$2,348.00	$1,695.00

$1,000.00 saved each year with an 12% return:

Years Saved	Total Saved with Interest	Monthly Payments 10 years	20 years
10	$ 19,655.00	$ 275.00	$ 208.00
20	$ 80,699.00	$1,129.00	$ 854.00
30	$270,293.00	$3,783.00	$2,861.00

 Action

1. At what age would you like to retire?
2. Do you qualify for social security benefits? If so, have you checked your social security estimates? If not, call and request an application.
3. Based on your current income how much should you save for retirement?
4. Do you know what your retirement benefits are? If not, make an appointment with your employer's benefits department and find out.

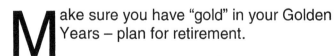

Make sure you have "gold" in your Golden Years – plan for retirement.

Chapter Ten
Finally! Financially Free

What does financial freedom mean?
Financial freedom is having enough money to reach financial goals without worrying. It is also the ability to manage money to get needs and wants.

How can females achieve financial freedom?
Ten ways to assist females in becoming and remaining financially free:

❶ Stay healthy
Your health is the greatest resource you have to reach goals. Poor health closes doors to opportunities that provide money to become financially free. Basic ways to promote good health include:

- Good eating habits – use the basic food groups as your guide.
- Keep your weight under control.
- Exercise – walk or participate in a daily exercise program.
- Get medical attention when needed – regular annual visits to the doctor and dentist should be part of your life.
- Be spiritually grounded – surround yourself with positive spiritual people and opportunities.

❷ Set realistic goals and learn how to achieve them.

Without goals you will never know when you have accomplished your aim. Your goals should say "u-smart."

U – Understandable. Goals should be clear and understandable. There should be no questions about what you are trying to achieve.

S – Specific. Goals should be specific. As you work toward them, they should continuously assure you that you are on track and should inform you when you are heading in the wrong direction.

M – Measurable. Goals should be measurable. They should tell how much or how long.

A – Action oriented. Goals should require some action. You should have to do something to achieve them. Goals are not accomplished without input from the goal setter.

R – Reachable and realistic. Goals should make sense and allow you success in reaching them. Goals are categorized as short-term, intermediate, and long-term. Short-term goals are those achieved in 3-6 months or less. Intermediate goals are achieved in 6-12 months. Long-term goals are achieved in one year or longer.

T – Time oriented. Goals should have an element of time attached to them. They should tell when you want the goal to become a reality.

❸Save and Invest

Financial freedom will depend on the ability to make your money grow. Saving a minimum of 2-6 months of household expenses in a savings account is the first step to successful investing. A goal of 10% each pay day is a great goal. Once saving is successful try investing in saving bonds or mutual funds. Savings bonds can be purchased for one half the face value and increase in value as they mature. A bond purchased for twenty-five ($25) dollars will be worth fifty-dollars ($50) upon maturity.

Example:

US Savings Bonds

Issue Date	Years to Maturity
Nov 1986-Feb 1993	12 years
Mar 1993-Apr 1995	18 years
May 1995-Current date	17 years

For bonds purchased earlier than dates on the above chart contact your local bank or visit the U.S. Bureau of the Treasury web site at: www.publicdebt.tras.gov

---

❹ Insure against risks

Purchase insurance to protect yourself from losses. Life, health, home owner, vehicle, and disability insurance will prevent you from having to lose assets if there is an accident or emergency. Most families cannot afford to cover losses with out-of-pocket money. Disability insurance should be considered. Research indicates that workers fifty years or younger are five times more likely to experience an employment disability than they are to die. Ask questions about any insurance before you enroll. Remember, term insurance is more affordable than whole life insurance and company group insurance plans are always more affordable than individual policies.

❺ Be comfortable with who you are

Low self-esteem and trying to keep up with others can be costly. Don't let others define who you are by what you have. Purchasing expensive name brand items to be seen or accepted can prevent you from having adequate funds to assist you in achieving financial freedom. It can also cause you to overuse credit to purchase items you cannot afford.

❻ Spend less than you make

The quickest way to see a financial difference is to spend less than you make. Develop a spending plan (budget) and set limits. Just because you have money left each pay day does not mean you need to spend it. Try saving and see what a difference it makes.

❼ Always be employable

Continue to invest in yourself even if you have a job. Education and job readiness are keys to being prepared for the job market. No jobs today are guaranteed. Employers can no longer expect employees to remain on the same job thirty years. Consider cross training and keep up with job market trends. You never know when your company will down-size, right-size or re-size.

❽ Plan your spending

Marketers spend billions of dollars each year studying consumers. As a result, consumers spend billions on impulse buying. Plan your spending. Make a shopping list and use it when you shop. Shop sales, eat before you shop, and shop without children.

❾ Be financially educated

Spend time each week financially educating yourself. If you want to understand how to achieve financial freedom, you must be committed to learning as much as you can about managing money, financial goal setting, and investing. Years ago managing money and investing was seen as a man's job. Today, women are sought after in the financial field. We have proven we can be successful in the investment world. Books, seminars, newspapers, radio and television programs are all available to help with financial education.

❿ Learn how to get more for your money

Be a creative spender. Learn how to get a job done with little or no money. Exchange services with family and friends. Use coupons and discounts. Remember, the more you save the more you have available to put toward your financial freedom goal.

Females must understand that financial freedom does not come over night. It will take time and commitment. Financial Freedom is earned. I am reminded of a speech given by Ms. Leah Dever, Manager, Oak Ridge Operations (July 1999) at a Federal Employed Women's luncheon. She focused on women, careers and success. Ms. Dever used the letters in the word **earn** to inform women how to achieve career success. Her information can be used to address how women can achieve financial freedom.

E – Education. Education should be an ongoing process. You are never too young or too old to learn.

A – Attitude. Your attitude determines how successful you are in anything you do. A good attitude will assist you in achieving great success; a negative attitude will do just the opposite.

R – Resumé. Be prepared and make sure your resumé gives others a clear picture of what you are capable of doing.

N – Network. Talk to others, learn to ask questions, and never isolate yourself from information.

 **Action**

Using the list of ten ways to achieve financial freedom, Identify three areas you will work on to move you closer to financial freedom.

1.

2.

3.

Each one help one. Make a list of at least eight females to share the information you learned in this book. Ask each person you share with to share with at least one other female.

1.

2.

3.

4.

5.

6.

7.

8.

With facts, females can make a financial difference in their lives.

Bibliography

Abentrod, S. *Beating Debt*. New York: Macmillan spectrum, 1996.

Blau, F.D. & K. L.M. *The Gender Earnings Gap: Some International Evidence*, National Bureau of Economic Research, December 1992.

Broussard, C.D., *The Black Woman's Guide To Financial Independence* New York: Penguin Books, 1996.

Brown, C., *Questions Every Working American Must Ask*. New York: Dearborn Financial Publishing, 1996.

Bureau of Census, *Money Income in the United States*, 1996.

Bureaus of Labor Statistics, *Employment and Earnings*, January 1998.

Dixon, C.S., & Rettig, K. *The Economics of Divorce: An Examination of Income Adequacy for Single Women Two Years After Divorce*. New York: the Haworth Press., 1995.

Dixon, C.S., Westbrook, E.M., & Bower, L.K. "Raising Credit Smart Kids." Journal of the Family Economics and Resource Management Division of AAFCS. Vol. 4, 1995.

Dixon, C.S., "The 10 Most Asked Questions About Bankruptcy." University of Tennessee Agricultural Extension Service Publication #SP457 (1995).

Feinberg, A. Downsize Your Debt. New York: Penguin Books, 1993.

Fronstin, P. "Sources of Health Insurance and Characteristics of the Uninsured: Analysis of the March 1997 Current Population Survey," EBRI Issue Brief Number 192, December 1997.

Garman, E.T., and R. E. Forgue. Personal Finance. Boston: Houghton Mifflin Co., 1997.

Godfrey, N.S. A Penney Saved. New York: Simon & Schuster, 1995.

Hayes. C.L. & Kelly, K. Money Make-overs. New York: Doubleday, 1998.

Institute for Women's Policy Research, the male-Female Wage Gap: Lifetime Earnings Losses, 1998.

Mishel, L., Bernstein, J., Schmitt, J. The state of Working American 1996-97, Economic Policy Institute, 1996.

Mosbacher, G. It Takes Money Honey. New: Harper-Collins Publishers, 1999.

O'Neill, B. Saving on a Shoestring. Chicago: Dearborn Financial Publishing, Inc., 1995.

Orman, S., *The Courage to be Rich*. New York: Penguin, 1999.

Orman, S., *The 9 Steps to Financial Freedom*. New York: Crown Publishers, Inc. 1997.

Pond, J.D. The *New Century Family Money Book*. New York: Dell Publishing, 1993.

Ramsey, D. *Financial Peace*. New York: Viking Publishing, 1995.

Ramsey, D. *The Financial Peace Planner*. New York: Penguin, 1998.

"Romance and Finance." Ebony Magazine, (February, 1999).

Scott, D.L. *Personal Budgeting*. Old Saybrook: The Globe Pequot Press, 1995.

Stanley, T.J., Danko, W.D. *The Millionaire Next Door*. Atlanta: Longstreet Press, 1996.

U.S. Census Bureau, Census Bureau Facts for Features. CB99-FF.03 (February 23, 1999).

U.S. Department of Labor, Employment Characteristics of Families in 1997.

U.S. Department of Commerce, "How Much Do Americans Save?" September 30, 1998.

Williamson-Harris, M. "7 Ways to Raise Money-Smart Kids." Essence (December, 1998).

Web sites
Financial Statistics. Youth spending:
www.rockymountainbankers.com/educ5.html

U.S. Treasury Department. Savings bonds:
www.publicdebt.

Teen Spending. News Release:
www.teenresearch.com

U.S. Census Data. Press Release:
www.census.gov/press-release/www/1999/cb99-130.html.

U.S. Census Data. Women's Earnings:
www.census.gov/hhes/income/histinc/incperdet.html

Women statistics - msn.com

Index

Order From
(Please photocopy)

I would like to order _____ Copies of *Financial Facts For Females*. The purchase price plus shipping and handling is $15.00 for each book ordered ($13.00 book cost and $2.00 for shipping and handling).

Please send book(s) to the following address:

Name: _____

Address: _____

City/State: _____

Phone: _____

Email: _____

Special Autograph to: _____

Send Check or Money Order to:
          Dr. Celvia Stovall
          P.O. Box 50296
          Raleigh, NC 27650-0296

Comments: _____

_____

_____

For group workshops or motivational speaking contact Dr. Celvia Stovall at: celvias@netzero.com